A Nation of Immigrants?

John D. Clare

HODDER
EDUCATION

The Publishers would like to thank the following for permission to reproduce copyright material:

Photo credits
p.4 © Gideon Mendel/Corbis; **p.9** *l* Roger T. Schmidt, *r* © alimdi.net, photographersdirect.com; **p.10** © Jon Arnold Images Ltd/Alamy; **p.12** © Lebrecht Music & Arts/Corbis; **p.13** Courtesy of Wikipedia Commons; **p.14** Courtesy of Wikipedia Commons; **p.15** © The Gallery Collection/Corbis; **p.16** © Detail from the Westminster Tournament Roll: College of Arms; **p.17** © Historical Picture Archive/Corbis; **p.18** © Mary Evans Picture Library; **p.19** © Illustrated London News Ltd/Mary Evans; **p.20** © Stapleton Collection/Corbis; **p.21** © Mary Evans Picture Library; **p.23** *l* © Paul Gapper/Alamy and courtesy of Dave B Savage (artist), *r* © Jewish Chronicle Ltd/HIP/TopFoto; **p.24** South Tyneside Libraries and Information Service; **p.25** © Shields Gazette; **p.26** © 2004 TopFoto; **p.28** *t* © Hulton-Deutsch Collection/Corbis, *b* © Hulton-Deutsch Collection/Corbis; **p.29** *tl* © Hulton-Deutsch Collection/Corbis, *tr* © Hulton-Deutsch Collection/Corbis, *br* © Hulton-Deutsch Collection/Corbis; **p.30** *tl* © 2001 Credit:Topham Picturepoint/TopFoto, *tr* © Hulton-Deutsch Collection/Corbis, *b* © Hulton-Deutsch Collection/Corbis; **p.31** *t* © Mary Evans Picture Library/Roger Mayne, *b* © Hulton-Deutsch Collection/Corbis; **p.32** © Getty Images; **p.33** *t* © Hulton-Deutsch Collection/Corbis, *m* © Hulton-Deutsch Collection/Corbis; **p.34** © Janine Wiedel Photolibrary/Alamy; **p.35** © Miramax/Everett/Rex Features; **p.38** *tl* © Rex Features, *ml* © FremantleMedia Ltd/Rex Features, *mr* © ITV/Rex Features; **p.39** *t* © Ken McKay/Rex Features, *m* © Rex Features; **p.40** www.CartoonStock.com; **p.45** *tl* © Burn Sisi/ArenaPAL, *tc* © Yellow Dog Productions, *tr* © Getty Images, *ml* © Stockphoto/PKFawcett, *mc* © Mike Abrahams/Alamy, *mr* © David Noble Photography/Alamy, *bl* © Jeff Crosby; **p.47** © Gideon Mendel/Corbis; **p.48** © Kent News & Picture/Corbis Sygma

Acknowledgements
p.5 Ipsos MORI, figures from MORI opinion polls (2008); **p.26** Aldwyn Roberts ('Lord Kitchener'), "London is the place for me ... " ; **p.27**: article on *Empire Windrush* immigrants from the *Guardian* (23 June 1948); **p.36**: Linton Kwesi Johnson, 'Inglan is a Bitch' (abridged) from *Tings an Times* (Bloodaxe Books, 1991); **p.37**: Kirti Joshi, personal story from *From There to Here – Sixteen true tales of immigration to Britain* (Penguin Books, 2007), selection © Penguin Books 2007; **p.41**: Simon Basketter, from article on immigration in *Socialist Worker Online* (23 October 2007) and James Slack, from article on immigration in *Daily Mail* (17 October 2007).

Orders: please contact Bookpoint Ltd, 130 Milton Park, Abingdon, Oxon OX14 4SB.
Telephone: (44) 01235 827720. Fax: (44) 01235 400454. Lines are open 9.00–5.00,
Monday to Saturday, with a 24-hour message answering service.
Visit our website at www.hoddereducation.co.uk

© John D. Clare 2010
First published in 2010 by
Hodder Education,
An Hachette UK Company
338 Euston Road
London NW1 3BH

Impression number   5 4 3 2 1
Year   2014 2013 2012 2011 2010

Cover photos: Immigrants from Jamaica arrive at Tilbury, London on board the "Empire Windrush", © Popperfoto/Getty Images; Westminster Tournament Rolls showing black trumpeter John Blanke, © Detail from the Westminster Tournament Roll: College of Arms.
Illustrations by Tony Jones, Steve Smith and Richard Duzczak (cartoons)
Designed by Lorraine Inglis Design in Imperial 11/13.5pt
Printed in Italy

A catalogue record for this title is available from the British Library

ISBN: 978 0340 957 721

Contents

Starter: Setting the question

First thoughts: A controversial topic

SOURCE 1

A male carer serves children a lunch of pasta with tomato ragù at the Sheffield Children's Centre, which provides daycare for children under five.

In 2004, an MP named Barbara Roche argued that immigration was a very good thing for Britain. One of the comments she made was directed at historians, who should, she wrote:

❝embrace our past as 'a nation of immigrants'. History should not be all about kings and queens, dates and battles, but should look at how immigration is firmly entwined with any notion of what it is to be 'British'. ❞

Barbara Roche, *Beat the Backlash* (2004).
In 2004 Barbara Roche was a junior minister in the Labour government.

So that is what we are going to do in this book.

As you study this topic, you need to be aware that this is a VERY controversial subject. It is a matter of fierce political debate – from those who believe that immigration is an economic benefit and a moral duty, to those who would stop all immigration and expel many of the immigrants who are already living in Britain.

It is also a very *personal* topic: you will be discussing traditions and truths which you and your classmates genuinely care about. There is a good chance you will be speaking in ignorance of many people's situations, and maybe even offensively. You will be talking about *their* family, and they will be listening not just to the words you speak, but to your tone of voice – they will be personally upset by any unkind words or careless gestures.

Britain today is deeply divided over the issue of immigration, and it is a conflict which (history has shown) can easily flare up into violence. There are laws in our country forbidding the making of racist or inflammatory statements. Therefore, we all need to choose our words carefully and be tolerant.

Immigration

An 'immigrant' is someone from another country who comes to live in Britain. There are many different kinds of immigrant here.

1. Any citizen of the European Union – a Polish plumber, for example – has the right to come and live and work in Britain (in exactly the same way that you can go to work in any other EU country).

2. Many people from outside the EU who come to live in Britain are 'legal immigrants', who have been given a visa for a temporary or permanent stay. They include:
    a) 'economic migrants', who have come to Britain to work (in 2003, the Home Office issued 141,000 work permits)
    b) 'asylum seekers', who ask permission to come to Britain to flee disaster, war or persecution in their own country. If their application is successful they are called 'refugees'; in 2003, the UK was thought to be hosting 289,000 refugees.

3. There are also 'illegal immigrants', who do not apply through the proper channels (for example, some are smuggled into the country hidden in lorries). One estimate in 2009 suggested that there might be up to one million illegal immigrants living in the United Kingdom.

SOURCE 2

- 59 per cent of the British public thought that 'there are too many immigrants'.
- 49 per cent of the public thought that immigrants should be encouraged to return to their country of origin.
- 76 per cent thought there was tension between the different races and nationalities living in Britain.

Figures from MORI public opinion polls, 2008. The polls were conducted by interviewing 1,000 people selected to be a representative sample of the British public.

Activities

1. Talk about Source 1 with a friend. What are its messages? Write your own caption to go with the picture.
2. Write down your 'First thoughts on immigration': do you think that immigration should be stopped, and why?
3. Discuss as a class the results of the public opinion polls listed in Source 2. What are your initial reactions?
4. Should the government be allowed to make history teachers teach about immigration? Explain your opinion.

CHAPTER 1

Mongrels or magpies?

Interpretations: Analogies for immigration

When talking about immigration, people sometimes use 'analogies' – images which suggest different things about immigration and betray their underlying feelings about it. Here are six analogies people use:

1 'A flood of immigrants'.

2 'Waves of immigrants'.

3 'A melting pot'.

4 'A salad bowl'.

5 'A mosaic'.

6 The 'bomb-shelter' analogy: the people in the shelter are safe, but how many more can it hold?

Activity

Consider the different analogies for immigration on this page.
a) What impression of immigration does each suggest?
b) Which analogies portray immigration as a bad thing, and which portray it as a good thing?

Knowledge: Immigration 10,000BC–AD1066

In the beginning

As far as we know at the moment, it seems that the land we know as Britain was uninhabited at the end of the last ice age, and was gradually populated after about 10,000BC by people who probably came from Spain.

Since those original settlers made their way across the land-bridge (which was later flooded and became the English Channel), Britain has been invaded and settled by unknown numbers of people who came to visit, trade, raid and conquer, and who have all made their mark on the nation's gene bank.

The Beaker people and the Celts

Around 2500BC, Bronze Age culture came to Britain with a group called the **Beaker people** (named after the kind of pottery they used). They seem to have introduced metal-working and the first alcoholic drink (mead) to Britain. We know little about how many of these people came to Britain, but historians think that only a few traders or conquerors came, bringing with them a new culture which was adopted by the existing population.

After about 500BC, people we now call the **Celts** brought the Iron Age to Britain. But whilst they caused great changes in the way people in Britain lived, historians disagree about whether there were large numbers of them. On the other hand, one guess is that there were barely 100,000 people living in Britain at the end of the Bronze Age so an immigration of just 5,000 Celts would seem like an awful lot of people.

The effects of the Celts can still be seen in some of our myths and traditions – our word 'bonfire' comes from Celtic 'bone fires', and 'druids' still meet at Stonehenge every year. The Celts are also credited with introducing the bagpipes and (maybe) horseshoes to Britain.

Can DNA tell us anything?

The first settlers of the British Isles, who came to Britain from Spain following the last ice age, had the gene type R1b. Recent DNA studies seem to suggest that none of the 'invaders' who arrived after these first Britons came in big enough numbers to affect the basic gene pool. The Angles seem to have affected South-East England, and there is Viking blood in the Orkney Islands, but the original gene type does not seem to have changed greatly: the English are 64 per cent type R1b, the Scots 75 per cent R1b, and the Welsh and the Irish more than 90 per cent R1b.

The Romans

The **Romans**, of course, 'came, saw and conquered' all of Britain except the highlands of Scotland. They invaded Britain in AD43 and stayed for some 400 years. The Roman policy of government was to 'divide and rule', so they garrisoned Britain with a mixed army of Gauls, Germans and Hungarians. There is also evidence that there was a settlement of black Africans near York.

But the Romans came for trade and taxes, not large-scale settlement. The entire Roman garrison was probably no more than 20,000 in a population of maybe 2 million, and the number of those men who took wives and stayed here is anybody's guess.

The effects of the Roman occupation on our way of life, however, have been lasting and significant. Much of our language and our laws can be traced back to the Romans, and many of our modern-day main roads are based on the Roman road system.

Activity

1. As you read pages 7–8, for each 'wave' of invaders, establish:
    a) WHEN they came
    b) HOW MANY came
    c) the lasting EFFECTS on our life today.

Saxons and Vikings

It used to be thought that **Anglo-Saxon** invaders from north-east Europe 'drove the Britons from the land' in the two hundred years after AD400.

However, historians now tend to suggest that, rather than coming in large numbers to settle, the invaders came in small groups and simply took over as rulers. One historian puts the number of Anglo-Saxon immigrants as low as 100,000 men at most, amongst a population of at least three million Britons.

On the other hand, the 'Angles' gave the English their name, and Anglo-Saxon is the base language of the English language. The thousands of place names ending '–ham', '–ton' or '–ford' suggest they had a huge impact on our country. The Anglo-Saxons laid the foundations of our laws and traditions, and we remember their gods in the names of our days of the week and their political organisation of the country in the names of our counties.

In the two centuries after AD800, the **Vikings** (from Norway, Sweden and Denmark) conquered Orkney and reduced the rest of the British Isles to trembling terror. They settled throughout the 'Danelaw' in the north of England, where their presence is shown in place names ending in '–by' and '–thorpe'. There are many archaeological remains of 'Viking Britain', for example at the Jorvik Viking Centre in York.

But again, historians believe that the Viking armies contained only small numbers of warriors, and that they settled in small groups as traders amongst the existing population. How much Viking blood runs in our veins is questionable.

Can DNA tell us anything?

Recent DNA studies of the gene type I1a, that of the Anglo-Saxons, seem to show that many English people possess this gene type, but that very few Welsh people do. Gene experts have said that this suggests that the Anglo-Saxons killed, or drove out of England, between 50 and 100 per cent of the Ancient Britons.

This contradicts the findings of historians, and also studies of the gene type R1b, which suggest that the actual population of Britain was not much changed by the invasions over thousands of years.

The Normans

The **Normans** arrived in very small numbers – although William the Conqueror's victory at Hastings in 1066 is regarded as the crucial turning point in our history.

The Normans revolutionised England. The entire Anglo-Saxon nobility was wiped out, and the whole structure of land-ownership was changed by the feudal system. Ten thousand words in our dictionary come from the French, and if you are called Roger, Stephen or Emma rather than Ceolfrith, Wulfhere or Ethelburga you have the Normans to thank. They invented surnames and they introduced fallow deer, pheasants, rabbits – and chess – into Britain. They changed forever our government, laws and class system, and some historians believe that they created 'Englishness' as a national identity.

Yet the Normans never amounted to more than 10,000 men, and – although many upper-class families today can trace their ancestry back to 1066 – it is questionable how many of the Normans contributed to the gene pool of the one million *ordinary* English people whose lives they changed so hugely.

Activities

2. **How far does the description 'made and remade by immigration' describe Britain in the years up to 1066?**
3. **How far is the phrase 'swamped by incomers' true of Britain in the years up to 1066?**
4. **Looking at the information on these 'early immigrants', which analogy from page 6 would you suggest best fits their invasions?**

Interpretations: Mongrels or magpies?

Recently, writers have suggested two other analogies for how immigration has affected the people of Britain:

SOURCE 1

SOURCE 2

Magpies

Not everyone likes admitting it, but one of the defining aspects of the national character may lie in Britain's historic ability to collect and absorb foreign habits, skills and people, even as it criticises them … We are … a magpie nation, quick to absorb and profit from foreign influences of all shades … We are all from somewhere else: it simply depends how far back you go.

Written by the journalist and historian Robert Winder, in his contribution to a government publication: *Britishness: Towards a progressive citizenship* (2008).

Mongrels

Bernardine defines the Britain she belongs to: not a 'myth version of British history, of a green and pleasant land – a deeply monocultural image of a Britain that's always been white'; but an 'island that's always been a mongrel nation, always settled by immigrants'. This, she says, is the 'Britain I choose to call home'.

A report about the black British novelist Bernadine Evaristo, who was speaking about 'identity' at a British Council conference (2003).

Activities

1. Write down in your own words what Robert Winder is saying in Source 1.
2. A magpie is a bird which is said to steal and collect shiny, attractive things. Is there any evidence on pages 7–8 to support Robert Winder's claim that the British people are 'a magpie nation'?
3. Write down in your own words Bernadine Evaristo's opinion in Source 2.
4. According to one dictionary, a 'mongrel' is a dog 'of mixed breed, arising from the crossing of different varieties'. Does the evidence on pages 7–8 support Bernadine Evaristo's suggestion that the British people are 'a mongrel nation'?
5. 'Flood'; 'melting pot'; 'mongrels' – can you think of YOUR OWN analogy to describe the influx of peoples into the British Isles in the years up to 1066? Explain how your analogy fits the facts.

Interpretations: Pre-historic foreign influences

The River Thames, showing Westminster Bridge and the Houses of Parliament.

The River Thames is one of our most famous national icons. In this poem for children by Rudyard Kipling, the River Thames – the only thing that has not changed through the centuries of invasion and immigration – remembers some of the changes it saw before recorded history:

SOURCE 1

I remember the bat-winged lizard-birds,
The Age of Ice and the mammoth herds […]
And I remember like yesterday
The earliest Cockney[1] who came my way,
When he pushed through the forest that lined the Strand[2],
With paint on his face and a club in his hand. […]
He fought his neighbour with axes and swords,
Flint or bronze, at my upper fords, […]
And North Sea war-boats, painted and gay,
Flashed like dragon-flies, Erith[3] way;
And Norseman and Negro and Gaul and Greek
Drank with the Britons in Barking Creek[4],
But the Roman came with a heavy hand,
And bridged and roaded and ruled the land,
And the Roman left and the Danes blew in –
And that's where your history-books begin!

Extracts from Rudyard Kipling's 'The River's Tale', written as the introduction to *A Schools History of England* by CRL Fletcher (1911).

1. A Cockney is a person who lives in London's East End; Kipling here uses him in the sense of 'the first Londoner'.
2. The Strand is a famous road in London.
3. Erith was a dock and industrial area on the south bank of the Thames to the east of London.
4. Barking Creek is where the River Roding joins the Thames; in the nineteenth century it was home to a large fishing fleet.

Activities

1. Consider the poem in Source 1. Divide the contents into three categories:
   a) content which is confirmed by the information on pages 7–8
   b) content which is contradicted by the information on pages 7–8
   c) content which is neither confirmed nor contradicted by the information on pages 7–8 – you will need to do extra research to prove whether it is true or false.
2. Write your own poem on the years 10,000BC–AD1066, based on pages 7–8.

2 Settlers from other lands

Knowledge: Immigration into Britain 1066–1900

In the centuries after 1066, large numbers of different kinds of immigrants came to live in Britain. This chapter looks in detail at five specific groups of people:

- the Jews (in the Middle Ages)
- the Huguenots (in the sixteenth and seventeenth centuries)
- the first black immigrants
- the Irish (in the eighteenth and nineteenth centuries)
- and the eastern-European Jews (at the end of the nineteenth century).

But there were many others. Before 1905 there were no laws to prevent immigration into England, and people came and went as they pleased. During the Middle Ages, Flemish merchants from Belgium set up businesses in many English and Scottish ports. Later, German merchants called the Hansa did the same thing – they had a huge dockyard called 'the Steelyard' in London. Occasionally, the king or queen would invite skilled tradesmen, such as German metal makers or Italian silk weavers, to come and set up businesses in England. After 1480 we hear of gypsy fortune-tellers coming over from mainland Europe. Flemish traders introduced gingham cloth. All these people had a profound effect upon our way of life.

Also, many upper-class immigrants were brought to England by the monarch to serve in the royal court; King Henry III in particular invited large numbers of French knights from Poitou to his court.

Many early immigrants were highly skilled workers. The German artist Hans Holbein was an economic migrant from Switzerland, who ended up as painter at the court of King Henry VIII. And in 1632, King Charles invited the Flemish painter Van Dyck to come to England to be the court painter. Other immigrants were refugees from foreign persecution, particularly in the sixteenth and seventeenth centuries when the Roman Catholic rulers of Europe began persecuting Protestants.

But the newcomers were not popular. In the early Middle Ages 'tournaments' – huge mock battles held for the fun of fighting – would take place and the knights often divided into 'English' v. 'Foreigners', at which times the fighting was especially bloody. During the Peasants' Revolt of 1381, the London mob looted and killed many Flemish merchants. Another example of this anti-immigrant feeling occurred on what came to be called 'Ill May Day' in 1517, when a mob in London rioted and looted houses in the foreign quarter (though nobody was killed).

Activities

1. Divide as a class into five groups. Each group takes one of the immigrant groups from pages 12–21 – medieval Jews; Huguenots; the first black immigrants; the Irish; eastern-European Jews – and uses the information to find out about the following questions:
   a) How many came?
   b) Why did they come?
   c) What did they do and did they prosper?
   d) How well did they integrate into the indigenous (existing) population?
   e) How were they treated? Were they persecuted/ discriminated against?
   f) How did they contribute to the British way of life?
   And finally, taking everything into account:
   g) Overall, how successful do you think this group of immigrants was?
2. Report your findings to the rest of the class.
3. Have a whole class discussion to decide to what extent the experiences of the five groups were similar, and whether you think England was a good place to come to in the years 1066–1900.

The medieval Jews

The **Jews** of the Middle Ages were one of the first groups to come to Britain after 1066.

Since they had been thrown out of Palestine by the Romans after AD70 the Jews had been a nation in exile. William the Conqueror brought some Jews with him from Normandy in 1066. They grew in numbers and prospered. Their children became doctors, goldsmiths, artists. They built synagogues and joined Christians in local businesses.

Some Jews became so important that we know them by name – Aaron of Lincoln, Abraham of York, Josce of London. Many of them made their living by lending money (something that Christians were forbidden to do in the Middle Ages). This made them both useful (because the Jews could lend money to people) … and hated (because they charged high interest rates). But our great medieval cathedrals could not have been built without Jewish loans, and Jewish money helped pay for the royal armies.

There were perhaps only 4,000 people in the Jewish community – 10,000 at most – in a population of around three million. However, there was always an underlying resentment of the Jews. They looked, dressed and sounded different. Many could read and write. People envied them their wealth and hated paying them back. They were not Christians – people accused them of taking part in evil religious ceremonies in which they sacrificed Christian children. When Richard I went on Crusade to try to conquer the Holy Land for Christianity there was a series of anti-Jewish riots. In York in 1190, 150 Jews were chased into the castle, where they committed mass suicide rather than be massacred.

After a while, when they ran short of money, English kings started simply taking money rather than borrowing it. King John fined the

This doodle from a medieval manuscript shows the devil pinching the noses of two Jews. What is the message of this drawing about the Jews?

SOURCE 1

Godeliva of Canterbury was taking some holy water in a wooden bucket, through the inn of a certain Jew. She went there at the invitation of a Jewish woman. For, being skilled in charms and spells, Godeliva was accustomed to charm the weak foot of the Jewess. But scarcely had she entered the hateful house when the bucket flew into three pieces and by the loss of the water she learned the wicked thoughts of her own mind, and – realising that she had committed a sin – she returned no more to that Jewess.

From a medieval chronicle, written c.1193.

The writer of the chronicle was a monk. What message was he trying to get across about the Jews?

Jews so much that many of them left Britain. One of them – a Jew from Bristol – was arrested and the torturer was ordered to pull out a tooth a day until the Jew paid £600; he lasted seven days before he did.

The Jews were forced to live in separated areas called ghettos. From time to time there would be riots when a mob would attack the ghetto and murder the Jews – always remembering to burn all the records of their debts at the same time.

The Jew's House in Lincoln dates back to 1150, making it the oldest occupied house in Europe. Aaron of Lincoln may have lived here. What does this house suggest about the Jews of Britain in the Middle Ages?

At first, the Jews survived because they had royal protection and support. As time went on, they lost that protection. During the rebellion of 1263–64, when Simon de Montfort temporarily overturned the power of the king, a mob rampaged through London and slaughtered the Jews. Jewish houses were looted in many towns, and some towns began to expel Jews altogether.

When he came to power, King Edward I issued the Jew Law of 1275, forbidding Jews from lending money and forcing them to wear a yellow badge.

In the years that followed, Jews were forbidden to worship (even in their own homes), to have Christian servants, to eat with Christians, to go out at Easter, or to work as doctors.

In 1287, Edward confiscated most of their wealth, and then in 1289 he arrested 680 Jews and put them in the Tower of London; 293 were executed. These were ideas which Hitler's Nazis were to copy eight centuries later.

Finally, in 1290, Edward solved his Jewish 'problem' by forcing all the Jews to leave England. One of the boats stuck on a mudflat and the captain persuaded his passengers to get off to lighten the load. Once freed from the mud he sailed off and left them to drown.

The Huguenots

After 1500, another group of immigrants started coming to England – Protestant refugees driven out by religious persecution on the continent. Large numbers of Protestants, called the Huguenots, came from France. The first Huguenots fled after many were massacred by the French Catholics in 1572; and immigration started again in 1685 when the attacks were renewed.

Tens of thousands of Huguenots escaped to England, more than 50,000 people into a population of six million – most of them going to London.

Perhaps because the newcomers were fleeing as refugees, or perhaps because they shared their Protestant religion, the people of England were at first kindness itself to the Huguenots, who settled and prospered.

The Huguenots were not impoverished beggars – many of them were successful businessmen in France, which at that time was much more advanced industrially and culturally than Britain. The new immigrants therefore kicked off that process which would, over the next century, 'transform England's agricultural economy into an industrial one'.

The Huguenots brought new techniques of wool dyeing, cloth printing, nail making and paper making. They set up silk factories and lace-making workshops. The Courtaulds family – who eventually set up the huge textiles firm – were Huguenots, as was Peter Dollond, whose optics firm would eventually become Dollond & Aitchison. And when the Bank of England was formed in 1694, a tenth of its capital was put up by Huguenot traders, and a quarter of its directors and its first Governor were Huguenots.

Finding themselves alone in a strange country, the Huguenots clubbed together and formed 'Friendly Societies', to provide for those who fell on hard times – the idea was to be adopted by English workers, and would eventually develop into the idea of the Welfare State.

Huguenot weavers' houses in Canterbury. Note that the houses have large windows to let as much light as possible into the workshops. What do these houses tell us about the Huguenots in seventeenth- and eighteenth-century Britain?

SOURCE 2

To all inhabitants of London this is to acquaint you that by forraigne nations wee are impoverished by them tradinge within our Nation especially by the French that is not all we may be fearfull of our lives first by theyr Rebellion in their owne land secondly by the fire and now thirdly by our tradinge but truly gentlemen now we are otherwise resolved for we will not suffer it noe longer … for wee will not have them raigne in our Kingdom.

From a paper issued by London apprentices, 1670.

What does this source show about the attitude of some British people towards the Huguenots?

The Huguenots brought with them new styles of French clothing which revolutionised English fashion. They also introduced lavender, the pressure cooker, oxtail soup, blancmange … and chips!

Finally, they played an important part in the history of Protestant Britain. They fought for William of Orange against Louis XIV of France and, when the Catholic Bonnie Prince Charlie rebelled in 1745, they pledged money and men to help defend London.

2 Settlers from other lands

Hogarth's engraving *Noon* (1736) shows well-dressed Huguenots leaving a London church, with poorer English people standing on the right. Notice the line in the middle of the road physically dividing the two groups. What did Hogarth think about the Huguenot immigrants, compared to the ordinary Londoners?

There was some fear about the 'swarme' of foreigners which led to occasional riots and attacks. French people were said to be 'of ill conversation and full of diseases', and were despised for eating snails and garlic. When King William of Orange suggested making them naturalised Englishmen, John Knight, MP for Bristol, likened them to one of the plagues of Egypt in the Bible: 'bringing forth frogs in abundance', finishing with a demand to 'kick foreigners out of the kingdom'.

Over time, however, the Huguenots merged into English society. They anglicised their surnames (turning, for example, Boursaquotte into Bursicott) and married English women. Their churches adopted the Anglican Church service.

Three-quarters of English people have some Huguenot blood in their veins, including the man voted the 'greatest Briton of all time' in a BBC poll of 2002 – Winston Churchill.

The first black immigrants

There had been black Africans in Britain during Roman times (see page 7), and in the Middle Ages Muslim black 'Moors' came to Britain from Spain. Later, large numbers of black Africans came to England during Tudor times as sailors, occasionally as traders, and often as slaves in the households of businessmen or nobles. By 1596 their numbers had swollen to thousands, and Elizabeth I wrote to the mayors of the towns complaining about the 'divers blackmoores brought into this realm, of which kind of people there are already here too manie', and ordering that 'those kinde of people should be sente forth out of the land' (she was ignored).

During the eighteenth century, English ships dominated the slave trade from Africa to the New World, and some of the slaves ended up in England. Many came as the servants of rich people, and they were educated and elegant. Historians tell us that there were 10,000 black Britons living in England in the late eighteenth century (in a population of about eight million).

It seemed to people at the time that this number was much higher: 'if they be not suppress'd, the city will swarm with them', worried the *Daily Journal* in 1723 – which was ironic considering that these African people had been brought to England as slaves; they had not *wanted* to come here at all.

Attitudes towards the black immigrants were mixed. A black servant – especially a black boy – was very fashionable, to be kept on show for visitors to see. Yet at the same time, black people were subjected to racial bigotry of the worst kind – dismissed as little better than orang-utans. They were accused of being lazy, criminal and immoral: Hogarth's *Noon*, if you look back at page 15, shows a black person kissing a white woman. Many black immigrants lived and died as servants, lonely and alone. Others, released into 'freedom', were forced to survive as beggars and prostitutes. Some were captured and put on ships to be taken across to the West Indies as slaves; one man beat this system by shooting himself. A few of the immigrants married white English partners but most died unmarried, and

A detail from the Westminster Tournament Roll (1511) showing a black trumpeter. There are several payments recorded in the accounts of the Treasurer of the Chamber to a 'John Blanke, the blacke trumpeter' (his name is a Tudor joke: 'blanke' means 'white'). He was paid 8d a day, and is an example of a skilled immigrant being employed by the monarch. What can we learn about John Blanke from this picture?

the numbers of black immigrants dropped quickly after slavery was abolished in 1833.

Nevertheless, despite the fact that they had been brought into the country as slaves, and were forbidden to take paid employment, some black Britons made amazing achievements.

Some took part in the fight to abolish slavery at the end of the eighteenth century. James Somerset set a precedent by successfully arguing in court that, as slavery was illegal in England, in England there could be no slaves. Black Africans such as Olaudah Equiano and Ottobah Cugoano formed themselves into a pressure group – the Sons of Africa – to fight for the abolition of slavery. Modern day historians now accept that black Britons played a significant part in the abolition movement – the first ever campaign to mobilise public opinion.

Some black servants were loved by their masters, educated, and remembered in their wills. One favoured black Briton, Ignatius Sancho, a valet to the Duke of Montagu, managed to buy his freedom and set up a fashionable salon, where visitors would sip tea and talk politics.

A black South African woman called Saartjie Baartman was tricked by a British doctor into coming to London in 1810, where she was exhibited in circuses as the 'Hottentot Venus'. Baartman was famous at the time for her prominent backside, but has become in modern times a symbol of the exploitation of black women. How does this shocking cartoon show people of the time treating her?

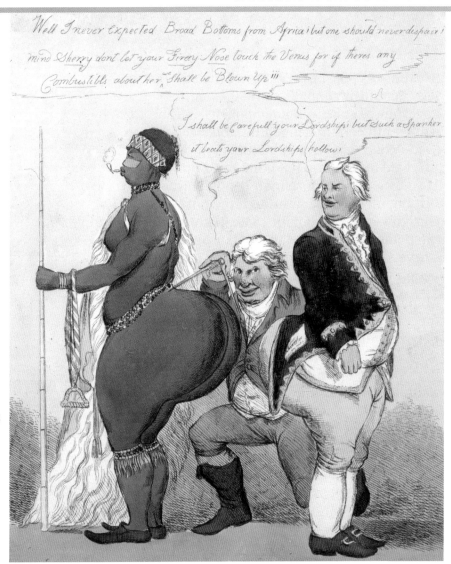

Well I never expected Broad Bottoms from Africa i but one should never despair i mind Sherry dont let your Firery Nose touch the Venus for if theres any Combustibls about her, shall be Blown Up !!!

I shall be carefull your Lordship i but such a Spanker it beats your Lordships hollow

In the nineteenth century, other black immigrants made their mark upon British society:

- Robert Wedderman (the son of a slave girl) campaigned for freedom of the press
- William Cuffay (the son of a slave) was one of the leaders of the 'Chartist movement', which campaigned for the vote for working men
- Mary Seacole (the daughter of a black Jamaican) paid her own fare to get to the Crimean War, and nursed soldiers on the front line, sometimes under fire
- Walter Tull (the grandson of a slave) became one of Britain's first professional footballers, playing for Tottenham Hotspur and Northampton, before becoming one of the thousands of black soldiers who fought (and died) for Britain in the First World War. He became the first black officer in the British Army to command white soldiers
- Samuel Coleridge-Taylor, the illegitimate son of a man from Sierra Leone and an English mother, was a brilliant composer.

The achievements of these people, given the racism and discrimination of the time, are little short of miraculous.

SOURCE 3

As a last resort, I applied to the managers of the Crimean Fund. But this failed also, and one cold evening I stood in the twilight. The disappointment seemed a cruel one. Doubts and suspicions arose in my heart for the first and last time, thank Heaven. Was it possible that American prejudices against colour had some root here? Did these ladies shrink from accepting my aid because my blood flowed beneath a somewhat duskier skin than theirs? Tears streamed down my foolish cheeks, as I stood in the fast thinning streets.

Mary Seacole describes her feelings after she had been rejected as a nurse in the Crimea, in her autobiography *Wonderful Adventures of Mrs Seacole in Many Lands* (1857). What did Mary Seacole blame for her rejection by the managers of the Crimean Fund?

17

The Irish

Ireland was part of the British Empire – part of the United Kingdom after 1800 – but the government's anti-Catholic policies in the eighteenth century ruined Ireland's economy to the point where large numbers of people survived on nothing but potatoes. From the 1790s, more and more Irish people migrated to Britain, most of them through the ports of Glasgow or Liverpool. In 1846, blight ruined the potato harvest: Ireland's poor began to starve, and hundreds of thousands of Irish people fled to Britain.

Many were so hungry or ill that they died on the short journey over the sea, or soon after they arrived. But others got work and survived. In 1861 there were 600,000 Irish-born people in Britain, in a population of 19 million, but this figure does not include all their children and descendants.

It is not true that all the Irish immigrants were poor, manual workers. One historian has found evidence of a small-but-thriving middle class of shopkeepers, midwives, landlords, schoolteachers … and even lawyers and doctors. In 1911, however, a census found that three-quarters of Irish-born males were unskilled labourers or farm workers.

Many Irishmen worked as 'navvies' (labourers) on the British canals and railways. They were wild, violent men who bought their beer by the gallon – men such as 'Crowbar Nobby', who used to sew up his lips to stop himself drinking, or 'Cat-eating Scan' who ran off with another man's wife and child. In many of the places the navvies passed through there was a spate of illegitimate births nine months later.

Elsewhere, Irish immigrants crowded together in areas of poor housing. One survey in Wolverhampton found a 'hovel' in which a man, his wife and child, and a donkey all slept in one room with a dunghill at one end. In one Irish area of Bradford, 1,453 people lived in 230 houses, sharing 435 beds and 36 toilets.

In such conditions, crime (much of it petty crimes such as stealing bread) and alcoholism

This affectionate view of a navvy, by John Leech, compares him to a soldier on the march. Leech trained as a doctor but made his living drawing illustrations for London magazines. He did not like capitalism and often showed rich people benefiting from the suffering of the poor. Was Leech typical of British people in his opinion of the navvies?

flourished, and the Irish were despised: in 1847 *The Times* called them 'a fetid mass of famine, nakedness, dirt and fever'; 'more like squalid apes than human beings', said the historian James Froude. The Irish were accused of taking jobs that English labourers could have done, and there were a number of anti-Irish riots, especially in 1846, which turned into small wars between the immigrants and the local people. For their part, the Irish communities sometimes responded to police raids by putting up barricades and rioting, and on more than one occasion the army had to be called in.

December 1891: 130 poor Irish are evicted from 'filthy, unwholesome and overcrowded premises' in Leather Lane, Holborn, London, on a cold winter's night. What attitude towards the Irish immigrants is being shown by the bailiffs in this picture? What is the attitude of the artist to the Irish immigrants?

The Irish were also hated because they were Catholics – they had to buy the land to build Catholic churches under false names, or people would not sell to them. They were also suspected of being traitors, especially after an Irish Nationalist bombing campaign in England in the 1880s.

There were further surges of Irish immigration in the 1930s, and through the 1950s and 1960s, and it continues to this day. Even in 1991, 3.5 per cent of London's population were born in Ireland. The 2001 census found that six million people (10 per cent of the British population) had Irish parents or grandparents – more people than the entire population of Ireland. One of the interesting facts about the Irish immigrants, however, was how few of them married Irish partners. Many married local men and women, and thereby quickly merged into the local population. In 2001, a survey by the Irish brewer Guinness found that 42 per cent of English people had some Irish blood in their veins.

The Irish, therefore, have made a huge contribution to Britain and its way of life. Famous Irish-born Britons include Oscar Wilde, George Bernard Shaw, CS Lewis, Dr Barnado and the Beatle George Harrison. Britain's canals, railways and roads would not have been built without them. Irish soldiers have long provided the backbone for the British Army – in 1830, the army was 40 per cent Irish. Irish immigrants have also fought for working-class rights, such as the Chartist Feargus O'Connor (who campaigned for the vote) and Ben Tillett (the great nineteenth-century trade union leader).

Irish dancing, Irish clubs and Irish religious processions have become part of British culture. The 'Scouse' dialect of Liverpool has been shown to be a mixture of Irish and English. Irish religious hostility between Catholics and Protestants has also followed the Irish immigrants, especially in Glasgow, where the Rangers v. Celtic derby matches are an echo of old rivalries.

The eastern-European Jews

This engraving of Wentworth Street in Whitechapel, London, in 1872 shows not only poor Jews, but other immigrants – Irish, Germans, French and Indians. From studying the engraving, what would you infer that Doré (the artist) thought about these immigrants?

King Edward I had expelled all the Jews from England in 1290, but in 1656 Oliver Cromwell allowed Jewish immigration into England once more. By 1850 their numbers had grown to about 50,000 (in a population of 18 million).

The Jewish community prospered. It included hugely wealthy families such as the Rothschilds, and in 1868 a Jewish man, Benjamin Disraeli, became Prime Minister. The Jewish community had its own newspaper – the *Jewish Chronicle*.

By the end of the nineteenth century many Jews living in England had become 'English' – many (like Disraeli, whose father was 'D'Israeli') had changed their names or (like Disraeli) had converted to Christianity.

At the end of the nineteenth century, however, the Jews of Russia and eastern Europe were suffering attacks (called pogroms) and large numbers of Jewish refugees fled for safety to Britain – 150,000 came in the years 1881–1914.

These new Jewish immigrants were not comfortable, wealthy and upper class like many of the British Jews. They were brutalised, starving and uneducated. Their condition was so terrible that women wept when they saw them.

Not everyone treated the new immigrants kindly. Jewish women were often tricked into prostitution. The Jews paid high rents to live in dreadful conditions in Whitechapel in east London. Inexperienced new arrivals – 'greeners' – were hired to work for impossibly low wages. Many went to work as tailors and seamstresses in the so-called 'rag trade' (making clothes in small workshops or at home).

A photo of Jewish immigrants in Whitechapel, east London, 1900. What impression of East End Jews does it give?

As more and more Jews arrived in London, hostility grew. English workers accused the new immigrants of taking their jobs, especially in the docks: the dockers' union leader Ben Tillett (see page 19) told them, 'Yes, you are our brothers, but we wish you had not come.' After 1892, the trade unions called for a complete halt to immigration.

These new arrivals were the first large-scale immigration of non-Christians into Britain. They looked different. They spoke Yiddish. They 'broke the Sabbath' by working on a Sunday. The poet Coleridge called them 'the very lowest of mankind'. Anti-Semitism (prejudice against Jews) grew into open hostility – it was at this time that the ideas which would eventually inspire Hitler's Holocaust were developed, by the Englishman HS Chamberlain.

The new Jews also faced hostility from the British Jews, who were worried that large numbers of Jewish immigrants would provoke a pogrom in Britain. The *Jewish Chronicle* urged the new arrivals to 'hasten to assimilate themselves immediately' (by which they meant they ought to become 'British' in their lifestyle) and declared: 'they are not Jews'.

But the Jews of the East End of London were far from the lowest of mankind. Most never drank, they worked hard at any job they could get, they took care of their children's education, and they were known as the most law-abiding people in the East End.

The contribution of these Jews to Britain's economy has been incalculable. One of the new immigrants, Michael Marks, set up the market stall which would eventually turn into Marks & Spencer. Another immigrant, Montagu Ossinsky, changed his name and set up the tailoring business which we now know as Burton Menswear. Jacob ('Jack') Cohen, the son of Polish Jewish immigrants, started a market stall, the name of which – after Cohen had been joined by TE Stockwell – became the acronym 'TESCO'.

But British Jews have made other contributions to British life. Siegfried Sassoon and Peter Sellers are just two famous names from a long list of British Jews in the cultural and entertainment world. 'Jewish comedy' has taught us to laugh at ourselves. And our word 'nosh' comes from the Yiddish word for a snack meal.

Knowledge: Twentieth-century immigration

The Aliens Act, 1905

The end of the nineteenth century saw a period of economic decline in Britain called 'The Long Depression'. It became very easy to argue that the large numbers of poor immigrants coming into Britain were taking British workers' jobs. Newspapers talked about 'a foreign flood', and the British Brothers League, formed in 1902, demanded: 'England for the English'.

As a result, in 1905, Parliament passed the Aliens Act. It was the first attempt to control the numbers of immigrants entering Britain. Introducing it, the Secretary of State, Mr Akers-Douglas, told MPs that the country was being overrun by 'destitute, diseased and criminal aliens from the rest of Europe'. The Act refused entry if an immigrant was ill or old, if he could not support himself and his family, or if he had a criminal record.

The First World War and after

When war broke out in 1914, Parliament passed the Aliens Restriction Act. For the first time in history, it defined what it was to be 'British':

- someone who (or someone whose father) had been born in Britain
- someone who had accepted UK citizenship
- a foreign woman who had married a British man.

Everybody else who came to Britain was an 'alien', and had to register with the police.

Large numbers of Germans had been settling in Britain throughout the nineteenth century, until there were 53,000 Germans in Britain in 1911. As soon as war broke out, however, almost 30,000 Austrians and Germans were sent home and 32,000 more 'non-British' people were interned in prison camps.

Newspapers called for 'a vendetta against every German in Britain', and a number of German-owned shops were attacked.

After the war, xenophobia (fear of foreigners) continued to grow. In 1919 there were a number of violent race riots in Liverpool, South Wales and London. The 1919 Aliens Act tightened the immigration rules, and further restrictions were added during the 1920s.

The 1930s

Immigration did not stop. An Indian community of seven or eight thousand grew up (a thousand of them were doctors). Black immigrants from Africa and the Caribbean arrived. They faced hostility and racism; it was almost impossible for a person with a black skin to get a room in a hotel or to go to a dance hall.

After 1938, 60,000 Jews fled from Nazi Germany to come to live in Britain – including brilliant scientists and wealthy businessmen. British Jews collected huge sums to try to help them, and many British people lodged Jewish refugees in their homes.

But when war broke out in 1939, seven thousand Germans were arrested and put into detention centres (including, ironically, a number of German Jews who had fled from Hitler). And when Italy joined the war in 1940, Churchill's response was to 'collar the lot' – thousands of Italian immigrants (including some who had lived in Britain for decades) were rounded up and imprisoned.

Activities

1. How was the Aliens Act of 1905 a 'turning point' in the history of immigration into Britain?
2. Draw a timeline for the years 1900–1940. Select FIVE important events mentioned on this page and label them on the timeline.

In the 1930s, while Hitler was persecuting the Jews in Germany, Britain had its own fascist movement, led by Oswald Mosley's British Union of Fascists (BUF) – nicknamed 'Blackshirts' – who held marches and rallies glorifying Hitler and taunting London's Jews. Unlike the Jews of Germany, however, the Jews of London decided to resist. When, in 1936, the BUF tried to march down Cable Street in the Jewish East End, the Jews and the Communists turned out against them. A forest of banners announced 'They shall not pass'. Barricades were built and the marchers were driven back – as were the police when they tried to help the marchers.

SOURCE 1

This mural was painted in the 1980s to celebrate the 'battle of Cable Street'. The original artist was Dave Binnington. He wanted to celebrate the victory over fascism. He researched the details of the battle very carefully by interviewing local people who took part in the event (he even included them in the painting). The mural has been vandalised and repainted a number of times.

SOURCE 2

An actual photo of events at the battle of Cable Street.

Activity

3. How useful is Source 1 for a historian who wants to study British attitudes to immigration in the early twentieth century?

Causation: The South Shields riot of 1930

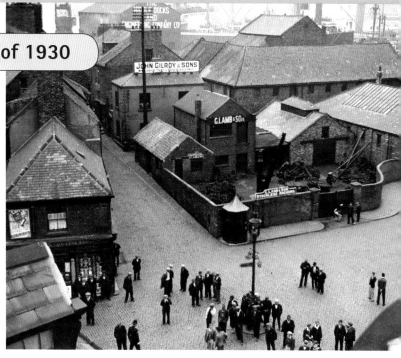

The riot

Arabs had been settling in South Shields since the 1890s – it is Britain's oldest Muslim community. They worked as seamen – usually doing the nasty jobs in the engine room – and thousands served on British ships during the First World War. Racial discrimination meant it was difficult to get lodgings in British ports, so a Yemeni Arab named Ali Said opened the first Arab seamen's boarding house in South Shields in 1909. By the 1930s, the Arab community in South Shields numbered about 3,000, mostly Yemenis and Somalis.

In the 1920s, however, the Yemenis suffered from the rules that the government introduced after the First World War. Although they had lived in Britain for many years, and had British wives and British-born children, they were told they had to prove their right to be in Britain, and many were deported because they could not find their documents. There was also a good deal of racist hostility towards the Arabs, especially because they were marrying white women.

Mainly, however, especially as economic conditions worsened, there were complaints about Arabs taking white men's jobs. In those days, out-of-work seamen would go to an area of the docks called Mill Dam to wait for work. In 1930, the National Union of Seamen did a 'British First' deal with the shipping owners which meant that Arabs would always be chosen last. On 29 April 1930, a group of Somali seamen were beaten up when they tried to sign on as firemen on a ship.

The Arabs campaigned against these rules. Helped by Communists and an organisation called the Seamen's Minority Movement (SMM), they held meetings and picketed the shipping offices in Mill Dam.

On 2 August there were meetings of the SMM, and tension was running high. The Yemeni

The Mill Dam area of South Shields, where the seamen used to go to seek work – showing warehouses, the offices of the shipping company, and a police box.

seamen were provoked by racist insults shouted by a white man named Hamilton. Then, when four white sailors were hired for work on a ship, a Yemini called Ali Hamid shouted: 'They work, but there is no work for the black man.' Fighting broke out. The police charged with batons and tear gas; the Yeminis drew knives and four policemen were stabbed. Six white men and twenty Yemenis were arrested.

After the riots, the white SMM organisers were each sent to prison for eight months, and the twenty Yeminis were sentenced to hard labour, after which they were deported. Ali Said, although he had taken no part in the riot, was convicted of being the cause of the trouble and deported.

Many more Yemenis who had taken no part in the riots were also deported. Others – with no work and no wages – ended up in the workhouse. A local newspaper suggested that 'since it seems impossible to send these people home, the next best thing is to segregate them', so the local council built a small housing estate nearby, on which only Arabs were allowed to live.

The causes

The South Shields riots of 1930 are often called 'race riots', but there is a great deal of disagreement about what caused the trouble.

SOURCE 1

The National Union of Seamen was built up by white sailors and firemen and [was] a growing concern long before the Arabs came here to deprive white men of work and gain for South Shields. My advice to these gentlemen, as they are too thick skinned to see that they are not wanted, is to get out while the going is good. I don't merely dislike Arabs. I hate them.

A letter in the *South Shields Gazette* (*c.*1930).

SOURCE 2

The press at the time played it up as a race riot. I'm against that. It was a riot for economic problems.

Darren Palmer, a third generation South Shields Yemeni whose grandfather was involved in the Seamen's Minority Movement in 1930. Darren was the director of a play about the riot.

A wounded docker is arrested.

SOURCE 3

It was a trade union dispute that happened between a union and another group trying to get equal pay for the Yemeni men and it kind of erupted. That's not a race riot.

Tina Gharavi, director of a 2008 exhibition which recorded the memories of South Shields Yemeni men. Tina was born in Iran and educated in the USA and France.

SOURCE 4

Efforts to exclude colonial seamen originated not with popular 'intolerance', but with employers who wanted them unprotected by union or social wages. *Agent provocateurs* provoked the Mill Dam riot of 1930 to destroy the Seamen's Minority Movement precisely because it organised across racial lines.

Laura Tabili, *Britain's Internal 'Others'* (2006). Laura is a social historian at the University of Arizona in the USA. An '*agent provocateur*' is someone – planted by the authorities – who provokes people to riot on purpose.

SOURCE 5

The Yemeni community in South Shields did not always find it easy … But things changed completely in 1930, after Yemeni workers protested against their working conditions. The relationship between Yemenis and their British neighbours improved considerably, and this relationship became a model of racial harmony.

British Ambassador Tim Torolt, speaking in the Yemen in 2009.

Activities

1. Read page 24 carefully. Think about what seems to have caused the riot. Make a list of causes, and then split them into 'long-term' and 'short-term' causes and what you think was the 'trigger'.
2. For each cause on your list, identify the facts which confirm it happened and then suggest an explanation of HOW it contributed to the riot.
3. Read Sources 1–4. Which of the four sources supports the idea that the riot was a 'race riot'? Look at the three other sources; what reasons do *they* suggest for the riot?
4. Look at the provenance of Sources 1–4. Which of the four authors do you think has most authority to comment?
5. Do any of the authors of Sources 1–4 have a motive to try to 'play down' the racism aspects of the riot? Explain why they might wish to do so.
6. Is Source 5 factually true? Why did Tim Torolt not tell the whole truth?

Now, taking all factors into consideration, discuss as a whole class:

7. Was the 1930 South Shields riot a 'race riot'?

25

Knowledge: *Windrush*

In 1948, the SS *Empire Windrush* was a troopship bringing soldiers and refugees back to Europe after the Second World War. On the way it stopped off at Jamaica, where it picked up 492 West Indians.

These were still the days of the British Empire, and there were no restrictions on any Empire citizen with a British passport coming to Britain. Tickets for the *Windrush* cost only £28, and many Jamaicans saw a chance to make some money working in the 'mother country'.

A number of them had fought for the British armed services during the war. All had been brought up to be proud of the British Empire, and full of admiration for the 'Land of Hope and Glory'. The difficulties they faced when they arrived in Britain, especially the racist hostility of many British people, cruelly dashed any illusions they might have had. On the journey to Britain they were segregated, for example they were made to sit in a 'blacks-only' area in the cinema. When they arrived, they faced a sea of posters saying 'Go Home'.

Privately, British Prime Minister Winston Churchill told the Governor of Jamaica that he feared that Caribbean immigrants would turn Britain into a 'magpie nation', which 'would never do'. He did not mean 'magpie' in the sense of Robert Winder – a nation which steals other nations' people and ideas (see page 9). Churchill meant that he did not want a nation which mixed blacks with whites, and he suggested fighting the next election on the slogan 'Keep Britain White'.

The *Windrush* immigrants landed at Tilbury in Essex on 22 June 1948. Most intended to make a little money and then go home. Many of them ended up staying for the rest of their lives. In time, they were followed by thousands more immigrants from the British Empire – the West Indies, Africa and India.

SS *Empire Windrush*

SOURCE 1

London is the place for me,
London that lovely city
You can go to France or America
India, Asia or Africa
But you must come back to London city

A song written by the calypso singer Aldwyn Roberts ('Lord Kitchener') on the voyage from Jamaica aboard the *Windrush*. Some of his later songs, such as 'White and Black', were about the racism he faced when he went to live in Manchester.

Evidence: Why 492 West Indians came to Britain

What were they thinking, these 492 men from Jamaica and Trinidad, as the *Empire Windrush* slid upstream? Standing by the rail this morning, high above the landing-stage at Tilbury, one of them looked over the unlovely town to the grey-green fields beyond and said, 'If this is England I like it'. May he and his friends suffer no sharp disappointment.

It was curiously touching to see against the white walls of the ship row upon row of dark, thoughtful faces looking down upon England, most of them for the first time. Had they thought England a golden land in a golden age?

What manner of men are these the *Empire Windrush* has brought to Britain? This morning, on the decks, I spoke with the following: a builder, a carpenter, an apprentice accountant, a farm worker, a tailor, a welder, a spray-painter, a boxer, a musician, a mechanic, a valet, a calypso singer, and a law student. Or thus they described themselves.

And what has made them leave Jamaica? In most cases, lack of work. Many can earn no wages. One man has been idle two years.

Most of the married men have left their wives and children at home, and hope to send for them later. Only five complete families sailed.

They are, then, as mixed a collection of humanity as one might find. Some will be good workers, some bad. Many are 'serious-minded persons' anxious to succeed. No doubt the singers will find audiences somewhere. So will the dance-band which is journeying to Liverpool at this moment. And the boxer, who is going to meet his manager at Birkenhead, will surely find fights in plenty. Not all intend to settle in Britain; a 40-year-old tailor, for example, hopes to stay here for a year, and then go on and make his home in Africa.

But the more worldly-wise among them are conscious of the deeper problem posed. In the past Britain has welcomed displaced persons who cannot go home. 'This is right,' said one of the immigrants. 'Surely then, there is nothing against our coming, for we are British subjects. If there is – is it because we are coloured?'

From a special correspondent of the *Guardian*, 23 June, 1948.

Activities

1. Using first the text on page 26, then the sources on pages 26 and 27, find at least TWO reasons why the *Windrush* immigrants came to Britain. For each of the reasons you have suggested, explain HOW it contributed to their decision to come.
2. Use Sources 1–10 on pages 28–31 to study 'the immigrant experience' for Caribbean immigrants in the 1950s and 1960s. For each photo, make notes on the following questions:
   • What is happening to the immigrant(s)?
   • How would this have affected the immigrant(s)?
   • What do you think the immigrant(s) would be thinking about this?

   Use your notes to imagine a fictional week in *your* life as a Caribbean immigrant, describing not only what you did and what happened, but also what you thought about it.
3. Compare the content and tone of Source 1 (above) with what you have learned on pages 26–31 about the reaction of many British people to the *Windrush* immigrants. Also consider the source's provenance and date. How useful is it to historians?
4. Based on your studies, do you think Britain should be ashamed of the way the *Windrush* immigrants were treated?

Research: Coming to Britain

The pictures and captions on pages 28–31 record the experiences of Caribbean immigrants coming to Britain in the 1950s and 1960s.

West Indian immigrants arrive at Southampton (1961).

Newly arrived West Indian immigrants at Victoria Station, London (1956).

SOURCE 3

A recent immigrant from Jamaica in the Clapham Shelter, London – a temporary hostel set up for immigrants who had nowhere to stay (1948).

SOURCE 4

Black workers outside the employment office in Liverpool (1949).

The original newspaper caption for this photograph read: 'Is There A British Colour Bar? Colonials are seen here outside the Labour Exchange in Liverpool. Apart from the city of Liverpool, it is fairly easy for coloured people to find unskilled labour in Britain.'

SOURCE 5

A recent immigrant to the UK from the West Indies reads the newspaper, perhaps looking for a job (1949).

SOURCE 6

Many immigrants – whatever their qualifications – ended up working in low-paid jobs such as hospital cleaners, on the underground, as bus drivers and conductors, etc. This West Indian ticket collector was one of 8,000 immigrants employed on public transport in 1958.

SOURCE 7

A young West Indian immigrant looking for accommodation reads a notice on a door which says 'No Coloured Men' (1958).

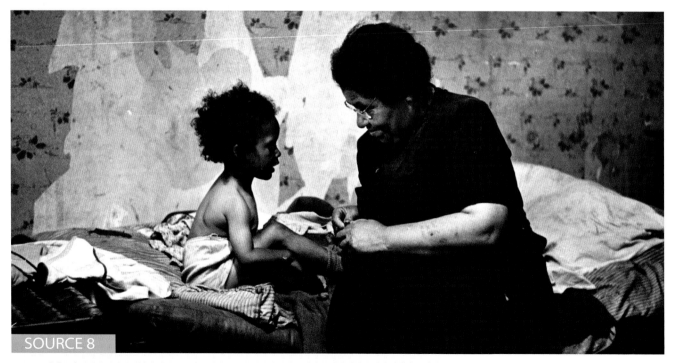

SOURCE 8

An elderly West Indian immigrant dresses a young child (1949).

West Indians in Southam Street, North Kensington, London (1956).

The photographer took this photo because it showed 'the melancholy, graceful West Indians, stepping out on a cautiously carefree prowl'. Newly arrived West Indian immigrants settled in and around Southam Street. The deprivation of the area, together with the influx of migrants, led to serious racial disturbances later that decade. The slum street was declared unfit for human habitation in 1963 and demolished in 1968–69.

It was unsafe for West Indians to walk the streets in this area of London at night; gangs of racist white youths would attack them.

Mr Siebert Mattison, a foundry worker who left Jamaica in 1947, sits with his Welsh wife and children in their one-room, Birmingham home. In the 1950s and 1960s, opinion polls showed that two-thirds of white Britons disapproved of mixed marriages. A lot of tension was caused by black men socialising with white women.

Knowledge: Immigration 1950–2000

Activities

1. Use pages 32–34 to discover FIVE Acts of Parliament which tried to limit immigration to Britain, 1962–93.
2. Find THREE key facts that could be used to claim that these were 'years of shame' for the British people and their response to immigration.
3. Find THREE key facts that could be used to claim that Britain responded positively to increased immigration.

At first the West Indian immigrants were welcome. As the economy prospered during the 1950s and 1960s, West Indian workers were actively recruited by both the government and private employers – especially the NHS, London Transport and the British Hotel and Restaurant Association.

Immigration from the 'New Commonwealth' (i.e. the black countries of the Commonwealth which had formerly been part of the British Empire) grew rapidly. Thousands of Indians and Pakistanis also came to Britain to work in the textile towns of Yorkshire and Lancashire, as well as Sikhs from the Punjab and Chinese from Hong Kong.

Many of these immigrants were single, and intended to go home after they had made some money. They were hard-working and prepared to work unsocial hours. Pakistanis became stereotyped for their 'corner shops', selling everything and staying 'open all hours', and by 1970 there were 1,200 Indian restaurants and 4,000 Chinese restaurants in Britain.

Tensions and restrictions

However, racial tensions – such as the Notting Hill riots of 1958 (see below) – frightened the government. In 1962 the government introduced the *Commonwealth Immigrants Act*, which brought in entry restrictions on Commonwealth citizens, allowing immigration only if the person had a work voucher giving permission to work in Britain.

Yet hostility towards the immigrants continued to increase. In 1964 a Conservative won the Smethwick Parliamentary seat from Labour with an openly racist campaign slogan: 'If you want a nigger for a neighbour vote Labour'.

◀ The Notting Hill riots started in August 1958, after white Teddy Boys – who had smashed West Indian clubs and harassed West Indian people – attacked a Swedish girl who had married a West Indian. West Indian youths armed themselves with knives and petrol bombs and fought back. The riots, which lasted five nights, consisted mostly of fights between police and white mobs who were shouting racist abuse and trying to attack the West Indians. Most of the 140 people arrested were white.

In 1967, a number of right-wing, Nazi and anti-Semitic groups came together to form the National Front. The National Front opposed immigration and encouraged racism. It grew rapidly until it had 20,000 members in 1974.

'Rivers of blood'

Then, in 1968, a crisis arose. Kenya (a Commonwealth country) expelled its non-black citizens and thousands of Kenyan Asians wanted to come to England. Worried, Parliament voted in the 1968 *Commonwealth Immigration Act*, requiring immigrants to prove a 'close connection' with the UK.

There was public alarm. In April 1968, a Conservative MP named Enoch Powell made a famous speech claiming that white British people were becoming 'strangers in their own country', looking forward to a time when 'the black man will have the whip hand over the white man', and predicting 'rivers foaming with blood' if the government continued to allow uncontrolled immigration.

Smithfield Meat Market porters march to the Home Office to protest about immigration, 1972.

National Front graffiti in London, 1968.

The Conservative leader sacked Powell, but opinion polls stated that up to three-quarters of British people agreed with him.

In 1971, the *Immigration Act* stated that only British citizens had 'right of abode' in Britain. This led to another crisis in 1972, when the Ugandan President Idi Amin expelled all 74,000 Ugandan Asians; in the end Britain agreed to take 21,000 Ugandan immigrants.

At the same time as it was trying to cut back on new immigration, the British government also introduced measures to try to prevent or reduce the black–white conflict in British society:

- The 1965 Race Relations Act made racial discrimination illegal, although it only applied to 'public places', and set up a Race Relations Board to encourage good racial relations.
- The 1968 Race Relations Act forbade racial discrimination in employment and housing.
- The 1976 Race Relations *Act* forbade all direct and indirect discrimination, and also set up the Commission for Racial Equality.

Moving towards a multi-racial Britain

The political debate about immigration continued through the 1970s and 1980s. Margaret Thatcher, who became Prime Minister in 1979, spoke about 'being swamped' and demanded 'an end to immigration'. In 1979, the Conservatives reduced the number of dependants who were allowed into Britain and in 1981 a new *Nationality Act* took British citizenship away from many New Commonwealth citizens.

In an attempt to stem the increasing numbers of illegal immigrants coming into the country, the government introduced heavy fines for anyone found carrying illegal immigrants – one consequence of this occurred in 1992, when a German captain threw overboard eight stowaways from Ghana, rather than pay the fine he would face on arrival in Britain.

An attempt was also made to reduce the number of asylum seekers. After 1993, the *Asylum and Immigration Appeals Act* turned away most asylum seekers, and imprisoned the rest in a detention centre whilst they underwent an investigation which might last for years. The Act did not allow them to work until their case was resolved, and forced them to survive on a grocery voucher and charity.

Nevertheless, the numbers of non-white people in Britain continued to grow steadily – from 400,000 (0.8 per cent of the population) in 1961 to 2.1 million (3.7 per cent) in 1981, and to 4.6 million (7.7 per cent) in 2001. By 2001, Britain had become a multi-racial country, with many different ethnic groups congregated in their own ethnic neighbourhoods – Banglatowns, Chinatowns, Little Indias, etc.

Total population	52,042
White British	46,879
Irish	642
Black Caribbean	564
Black African	480
Asian	
Indian	1,037
Pakistani	715
Bangladeshi	281
Chinese	227
Mixed	505

Some of the main ethnic groups in Britain in 2001 (in '000s)

Cultural clashes

The presence of growing but separate ethnic communities created cultural tensions. In 1981 there were serious race riots in Brixton and Southall in London, and in Toxteth in Liverpool. There were more race riots in Bradford in 1995, and in Oldham and Burnley in 2001. Reports about these disturbances blamed the segregated, 'fractured societies' in the towns.

Neither was the tension simply between the ethnic communities and the white population. In Birmingham in 2005 there were two nights of fighting between black British (African-Caribbean) and British Asian (Pakistani and Bangladeshi) youths. A study of the city found racism not only in the white community towards the non-whites, but between the minority racial groups.

In these circumstances, immigrants tried to settle down and bring up their children – children, of course, who had been born in Britain and regarded themselves not as 'immigrants', but as 'black British' or 'British Asian', etc.

Using evidence: Assimilation and its problems

Many of the immigrants who came to Britain (especially in the 1950s and 1960s) moved into the existing white communities. They – and particularly their children – often actively tried to merge into the British population, and this led to tensions within immigrant families.

The play (and film) *East is East* tells how this story was played out in the family of George Khan, a Pakistani immigrant to Salford in Lancashire.

George Khan's problems

1. He is married to a white English woman, but he has a 'Number One' wife back home in Pakistan whom he never sees.
2. His eldest son Nazir, who is gay, runs away rather than marry his (arranged) bride.
3. His youngest son Sajid won't have a bath and won't take off his anorak, and is found to be uncircumcised.
4. His daughter Meenah is wild and a tomboy and not the modest Muslim girl he would like her to be.
5. His son Tariq likes nightclubs, drinks alcohol and is dating a white girl.
6. His children secretly eat bacon and take part in the local Catholic Church parades.
7. He is ashamed of his children because they cannot speak Urdu.
8. His son Salim wants to be an artist and makes rude sculptures.
9. He tries disastrously to arrange marriages for two of his sons to two very ugly Muslim girls from Bradford.

Set in 1971, *East is East* is a drama about domineering father George Khan, who yearns to have an orthodox Muslim family but finds that he is constantly thwarted. The title derives from a poem by Rudyard Kipling: 'East is East, and West is West, and never the twain shall meet' – the joke, of course, is that they HAVE met, in Salford in Lancashire, and the film is about the resultant tensions and disappointments.

SOURCE 1

In the early years before hordes of Punjabis arrived, my mother dressed us like the English. My brother and I associated with English friends. As our parents did not want us to be different in any way, they made sure we learned English properly. When our relatives came, everything changed. The women would come to our house and say, 'Don't you think Nimi's hair should be braided now that she is ten?' or 'Nimi should not go to school with bare legs, otherwise she will grow up to be immodest.' Immediately my mother's attitude changed. I was no longer to be like the English, but was to dress and be like the Punjabi villagers, whom I began to hate.

A Sikh woman – Nimi – remembering her experiences in 1979.

Activities

1. Use the information on this page to list some of the problems faced by immigrants coming to live in Britain.
2. Explain how Source 1 mirrors some of the issues raised in the film, *East is East*.
3. How can you tell that Nimi was hostile to the recently arrived immigrants and the cultural effect they had upon her life?

SOURCE 2

w'en mi jus' come to Landan toun
mi use to work pan di andahgroun
but workin' pan di andahgroun
y'u don't get fi know your way aroun'

mi get a lickle jab in a big 'otell
an' awftah a while, mi woz doin' quite well
dem staat mi aaf as a dish-washah
but w'en mi tek a stack, mi noh tun clack-watchah!

*Inglan is a bitch – dere's no escapin' it
Inglan is a bitch – dere's no runnin' whey fram it*

w'en dem gi' you di lickle wage packit
fus dem rab it wid dem big tax rackit
y'u haffi struggle fi mek en's meet
an' w'en y'u goh a y'u bed y'u jus' cant sleep

mi use to work dig ditch w'en it cowl noh bitch
mi did strang like a mule, but, bwoy, mi did fool
den awftah a while mi jus' stap dhu ovahtime
den aftah a while mi jus' phu dung mi tool

well mi dhu day wok an' mid dhu nite wok
mi dhu clean wok an' mid dhu dutty wok
dem seh dat black man is very lazy
but it y'u si how mi wok y'u woulda sey mi crazy

dem have a lickle facktri up inna Brackly
inna disya facktri all dem dhu is pack crackry
fi di laas fifteen years dem get mi laybah
now awftah fiteen years mi fall out a fayvah

mi know dem have work, work in abundant
yet still, dem mek mi redundant
now, at fifty-five mi gettin' quite ol'
yet still, dem sen' mi fi goh draw dole

**An abridged version of the poem 'Inglan is a Bitch',
by Linton Kwesi Johnson (1980).**

**Linton Kwesi Johnson was born in Jamaica in 1952. In 1963 he
came to London, where he went to school and then to university.
Whilst still at school he joined the radical black group the 'Black
Panthers', helped to organise a poetry workshop within the
movement and started to work with poets and musicians. He is
known as the world's first reggae poet.**

**This poem does not tell Johnson's own story, but that
of many Caribbean immigrants of the 1950s and 1960s.**

Activities

4. Compare the two sources on pages 36 and 37. In what ways are they similar? In what ways are they different?
5. What impressions do the sources give of an immigrant's experience in coming to live in Britain?
6. The *Windrush* immigrants got jobs easily, but mainly in low-skilled occupations, and they faced poor housing, discrimination, racism and violence (see pages 26–31). List the similarities and differences of Kirti Joshi's experience on page 37. Had *anything* improved?
7. Using all the evidence, make a list of the 'downsides' and the 'upsides' of the immigrants' experience.

I came to England on 26 September 1972. I felt very lucky because I found a place to rent in Shepherd's Bush, west London. The house was damp and cold, but I couldn't complain. A lot of landlords didn't want to rent their houses to Ugandan Asians.

I got some good news at last. My elder brother got in touch with me and told me that he was living in a place called Leicester. I had read about Leicester. The City Council was discouraging the Asians from settling there. My brother found me somewhere to live in an area called Belgrave [and] got me a job at the factory where he worked. For the first time, I didn't feel isolated or abandoned, even though I had travelled thousands of miles to the UK. However, I can still recall the newspaper headlines of that time: 'New flood of Asians to Britain' and 'Enough of Asian influx'.

I lived as simply as I could. England was my home now and life went on. I didn't feel too isolated with so many Asians living in Belgrave. I knew Asians who were living in different parts of Leicester. When I listened to their stories of racial abuse, I was glad I was living in Belgrave, though I did experience a great deal of abuse myself. I witnessed people having glasses smashed in their faces, getting stabbed and generally being harassed.

My job at the factory was secure. I felt I had some stability in my life. My son was born in 1977 and I was a very happy man. The only downside was the racial tension growing in Leicester. I'll never forget the rival gangs on opposite pavements. The letters 'KBW' were scrawled in many places; I was told that this stood for 'Keep Britain White'. At times like these, I used to wish I were back in Uganda. I didn't want to be a burden to this country. During the mid to late 1970s, the National Front became increasingly popular. Violent clashes became common. I witnessed the riot in Leicester in 1981. It was frightful and horrifying.

From 1983, I found racial tension was declining. My children were growing up and it seemed to me that everything started changing very fast. It was quite remarkable for me to watch my children embrace British culture. My daughters wanted freedom to socialise with their friends from college. Looking back now, I do realize how confusing it must have been for them; it was just as bewildering for me. In Uganda, we had been a close-knit family; it seemed that once we left we separated and went our own ways … the closeness is not there.

Numerous Asian restaurants opened, alongside sari, gold and grocery stores. Diwali and other significant festivals were being celebrated. The Working Men's Club even introduced 'Asian nights'. Every now and again, my thoughts went back to Uganda. I remember watching a video that my friend took of Uganda when he went to visit. The place looked modern and peaceful. Halfway through watching, my wife walked out of the room in tears. Sometimes when I'm on my own and I think of my life in Uganda, I can't help but cry.

It is now 2007 and I can honestly say that I am very happy to be living in England. I will always hold this country in high regard; it was the country that gave me salvation. The first few years of living here were horrendous, but as time went on things changed for the better. I know racism is still widespread but it is not as bad as it used to be. I'm pleased to see so many people in mixed-race relationships.

I'm not living in fear and I have freedom. I'm proud to be living in a multicultural city. I'm indebted to the British government. The British Asian Uganda Trust is a charity that raises money for British charities as a way of saying 'thank you' to Britain.

Kirti Joshi was one of the Ugandan Asians expelled from Uganda by Idi Amin (see page 33).

This is his personal story of coming to England, remembered in 2007.

Interpretations: Race on the television

SOURCE 1

Alf Garnett, the lead character in TV's *'Till Death Us Do Part* (1965–75) loved the Queen and the Empire, but hated Communists, Jews, gays, the Labour Party … and his daughter's long-haired, unemployed husband. He resented black immigrants, used racist abuse-words when referring to them, and spoke approvingly about Enoch Powell in a number of episodes.

Alf Garnett was ridiculously extreme – he hated *everybody*. But he was pathetic and always ended up losing. The writer, Johnny Speight, used him to turn people against his views.

'Till Death Us Do Part did not see itself as racist, but nowadays the script seems horrifically racist. Warren Mitchell, the actor who played Alf Garnett, was both a Jew and a Socialist and hated the character he had to play.

SOURCE 2

The comedy of *Love Thy Neighbour* (1972–76) was based around what happened when a black couple moved in next door to a white couple.

Eddie Booth was a Socialist. His new neighbour, Bill Reynolds, was a West Indian Conservative. Both men were racist, and used racist abuse-words when referring to each other.

At the time, the show was presented as an attempt to heal the racial divide; both men were stupid and ridiculous, and they bore each other no hatred. Their wives got along very well. The black character Reynolds usually came out the winner in his ridiculous conflicts with Booth.

Today, however, the open racism is embarrassing and the show rarely appears on TV.

SOURCE 3

The comedy *Rising Damp* (1974–78) was based on a snooping, paranoid landlord, Rigsby, and the tenants who lived with him.

There is no doubt that Rigsby voiced racist comments and opinions about his black lodger, Philip, but it was clear that Rigsby was a ridiculous, laughable character.

By contrast, Philip (who in the opening episodes was presented as an African prince) was always calm, sensible, polite and educated – in fact, he was the only character who was not inadequate in one way or another. Miss Jones yearned after Philip, and was oblivious to his skin colour.

Rising Damp is regularly repeated on TV and is still popular.

The TV sketch series *Goodness Gracious Me* (1998–2001), featuring four Asian actors, was a conscious parody of white attitudes towards Asians. One of the most famous sketches was 'Going out for an English', which showed drunk Asians going to an English restaurant after a night's drinking, mispronouncing the waiter's name, choosing the blandest food, sexually harassing the waiter and ignorantly ordering far too much food.

The show also poked fun at British Asians – for instance the sketch in which 'Mr Everything-comes-from-India' tried to convince his daughter that Santa Claus comes from India.

Jade Goody (left) became popular for her loud-mouthed ignorance on the 2002 *Big Brother* series. Goody's father, who was of Jamaican descent, left home when she was two and died of a heroin overdose.

Going into the *Big Brother* house a second time in 2007, Jade (with two other housemates) caused outrage by making bitchy remarks about the beautiful and elegant Indian actress Shilpa Shetty (right), including calling her 'Shilpa Poppadom'. The programme received 40,000 complaints, and crowds in India burned effigies of Jade Goody. After the series, police interviewed Jade relating to the Race Relations Act.

Before the racism row, Jade was a UK celebrity; the affair ruined her career. Shilpa Shetty – a B-list Bollywood star – won the series and became famous.

Activities

1. Study Sources 1–5. For each source, discuss:
   - How did it portray the non-white community?
   - Was it racist (and what is the evidence)?
   - Should it be banned today (and why)?
2. Does Source 1 prove that the British people in the 1960s were racists who hated immigrants?
3. If we accept that television must reflect to some extent the attitudes of the society which watches it, what does Source 2 suggest about British attitudes to race in the 1970s?
4. Why, when *Love Thy Neighbour* is rarely shown on TV today, do people still watch *Rising Damp*?
5. What does Source 4 tell us about British attitudes to race at the turn of the century?
6. What does Source 5 show us about how the portrayal of immigrants on TV has changed/ developed over the period 1965–2007?

Using evidence: Is immigration a problem?

1965–70	– 250
1970–75	– 285
1075–80	– 50
1980–85	– 250
1985–90	30
1990–95	170
1995–2000	490
2000–05	945

◀ **Net migration into the United Kingdom, 1965–2005 (thousands).**

Net migration is the final change in population after all the people leaving to live abroad (emigrants) and all the people coming to live in Britain (immigrants) have been taken into account.

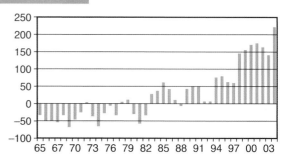

A graph showing net migration to England, 1964–2003.

More and more people have been coming to live in Britain. In 2005, for example, 565,000 people came to the UK. They included:

1. legal immigrants, including:
   • 137,000 people with work permits
   • 46,000 wives and children legally allowed to come to Britain

2. at least 212,000 citizens of the European Union legally allowed to come to work in Britain

3. 25,710 applicants for asylum (although only 10,760 were officially allowed to stay, many of those refused asylum remained in the country illegally)

4. and an unknown number of illegal immigrants.

In 2005, 217,000 people applied to become UK citizens, of whom 162,000 were accepted. This rate of immigration is equivalent to adding a city the size of Peterborough to the UK population every year – with all that means for housing, education and the health and welfare services.

'Bloody immigrants! You come over here and fix our leaking sink...'

After the EU was expanded in 2004, many workers from eastern Europe were able to come to Britain to work. Almost a million came to Britain 2004–08; almost half of them from Poland. Many were skilled tradesmen – the myth of 'the Polish plumber' grew up, although only 95 had actually registered as such.

Activities

1. Present Source 1 as a graph, and explain Source 2 in words.
2. What point is the artist of the cartoon in Source 3 trying to make?

3. '… with all that means for housing, education and the health and welfare services'. Discuss as a class the implications – positive and negative – of large-scale immigration on these four services.

The Migration Impacts Forum (MIF)

In 2007, the MIF collected the 'feelings' of eight groups of local government officers. Its report found the following:

- overall, immigration benefited the UK
- all regions noted the good work attitude of immigrants; jobs like farming and care-work depended on immigrant workers. The North-West region noted that 13 per cent of National Health Service staff were immigrant workers
- four regions had noticed increased pressure on housing
- five regions noted increased numbers of children who did not speak English
- two regions mentioned increased pressure on doctors
- two regions reported some increase in community tension
- five regions noted increases in some low-level crime (e.g. not using a seat belt)
- many regions were worried that the immigrants were being cheated by greedy employers and landlords.

Government finally admits: Immigration IS placing huge strain on Britain

IMMIGRANTS are placing a huge strain on public services, Labour finally admitted.

Crime is up, schools are struggling to cope with eastern European children, community tensions are rising, health services are coming under enormous pressure and house prices are being driven up, the Government said.

The findings, based on a survey of public sector workers, are the first published by ministers after ten years of an 'open door' immigration policy.

- The expert's verdict: Influx costs every UK household £350 a year.

From an article by James Slack in the *Daily Mail* newspaper (17 October 2007).

The *Daily Mail* opposed immigration and often criticised the Labour government of the time.

The claim that immigration cost £350 per household was not made in the MIF report, but by an Oxford professor in an entirely different paper.

Report shows benefits of immigration into Britain

The right-wing claim that immigration leads to job losses and lower wages took a blow last week from a Home Office report … The *Economic and Fiscal Impact of Immigration* report … said the increase of migrant workers in the workforce contributed £6 billion to the economy last year.

Another Home Office report last week talked about the strain on services caused by migration. This was a survey of attitudes rather than of evidence. It is not surprising that, as the government makes cuts to public services, people feel that there is a crisis in health and education.

But the survey noted that 13 per cent of NHS staff in the North West of England are immigrants. Migrants are not straining resources, but rather working alongside non-migrant workers in providing services.

From an article by Simon Basketter in the *Socialist Worker Online* newspaper (23 October 2007).

The *Socialist Worker* opposes the right-wing politicians who want to stop immigration.

Activities

4. Is the author of Source 4 for or against immigration? What points does he make to prove his point?
5. How accurate is Source 4 in its portrayal of the Migration Impacts Forum report? Use the information box on the MIF to evaluate the reliability of the CONTENT of Source 4, then use the provenance of Source 4 to assess the author's PURPOSE.
6. Is the author of Source 5 for or against immigration? How does he prove his point?
7. How accurate is Source 5? Evaluate the reliability of the CONTENT of Source 5, then use the provenance of Source 5 to assess the author's PURPOSE.
8. Both Sources 4 and 5 include additional information which did not appear in the MIF report. What extra information did they include, and why?
9. Does Source 3 agree most with Source 4 or Source 5? Explain your answer.

Knowledge: What have the immigrants ever done for us?

The impact of immigration upon Britain and the British way of life has been huge. In 2009, one in nine of the people living in Britain – and one in three of the people living in London – was born abroad. One in seven primary school pupils did not speak English at home. Britain is now the home of people from dozens of different ethnic cultures.

The diversity of life and lifestyle in our country today is something which enriches all our lives, and makes them more interesting and exciting. It is difficult now to find an aspect of life in Britain that has not been affected by and merged with other cultures. The character of 'British culture', it could be argued, is that it is now 'multi-cultural'.

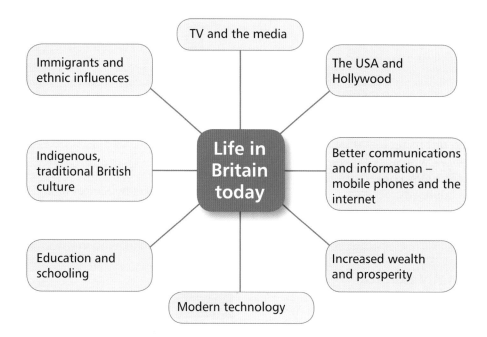

British culture is changing all the time. This spidergram shows some of the factors which are influencing our 'British way of life' today.

Activities

1. Study the illustration on page 43 which shows the contribution of immigrants and ethnic influences to life in Britain today. How many of them directly affect you? Divide the factors into economic, social and cultural effects (some might appear in more than one category).

2. Using pages 42–43 – and also the previous pages in this book, internet research and your personal experience – can you think of any other ways that life in Britain today is affected by immigrant and ethnic influences?

3. Select TWO important immigrant and ethnic influences and explain to a friend what your life would be like without these things.

4. Look at the spidergram (above) of influences which are changing British culture today. Discuss them with a friend, identifying at least one way – something you do or have or think – in which each influence has affected YOUR life. Use your judgement to list them in 'order of impact' upon the British way of life today.

In 2006 there were 1.6 million Muslims living in Britain; the same number of people as regularly attended a Church of England service.

Sport – notably football, cricket, athletics and boxing – is an area of British life where both British- and foreign-born black and Asian players are fully integrated and successful.

Ethnic influences have affected dance and music, with the advent of such genres as reggae, rap and bhangra.

The NHS has been particularly reliant on immigrant workers; in 2003 almost 30 per cent of the total number of doctors employed in the UK were foreign-born.

From the 1970s, fashion has been affected by ethnic influences.

In 1990 there were 15,000 corner shops run by Indian, Pakistani or Bangladeshi shopkeepers.

More than 200 different languages are spoken in Britain today.

One in seven of the British workforce today was born in another country.

In 2008 there were 8,500 Indian restaurants and 14,000 Chinese takeaways.

Reflection: What is 'Britishness'?

On 7 July 2005, four bombs exploded on London tube trains and a bus, killing 52 people. The public were alarmed to find that, of the four Al Qaeda bombers, only one was an immigrant (from Jamaica) – the other three had immigrant parents, but had been born and had grown up in Britain.

This unleashed a fierce debate about what was happening in British society to alienate young Muslims to the point that they were prepared to do such a thing. How should British society respond to the growing ethnic communities, to stop such a thing happening again in the future?

In 2006, Gordon Brown (the Chancellor at the time, but later to become Prime Minister) addressed the issue raised by the 7 July bombers:

> *We have to face uncomfortable facts that they were British citizens, British-born … who were prepared to maim and kill fellow British citizens irrespective of their religion. We have to find the essential common purpose without which no society can flourish.*

Coming up with ideas

The way to find this common purpose, said Gordon Brown, was by promoting 'Britishness', and he invited people to identify our shared common values and to think of ways to celebrate being British.

The challenge appealed to people, who came up with a long list of characteristics of 'being British'. Many suggestions were superficial or comic.

Other more serious people pointed out that Britishness for an old age pensioner in Somerset would be very different from Britishness for a black teenager in London. One London teacher thought the whole idea was racist – an excuse to impose a white view of Britishness.

Losing identity

When the Commission for Racial Equality asked a large number of people in 2005 what they thought Britishness was, it found that rather than trying to define Britishness, many white British people instead merely complained that they felt Britishness was in decline. This finding was reinforced by a 2008 MORI public opinion poll, which found that 58 per cent of British people agreed with the statement: 'Parts of this country don't feel like Britain any more because of immigration'. Many white British people seemed to think that multiculturalism was undermining a sense of what it was to be British.

British citizenship

In 2005, the British government decreed that anyone applying to become a British citizen ('naturalisation') or to settle in Britain ('indefinite leave to remain'):

1. had to have an ESOL (English for Speakers of Other Languages) qualification, and

2. had to pass a 'Life in the UK' test based on a factual booklet *Life in the United Kingdom*. The questions were difficult, and many British people who have lived here all their lives would find it hard to pass the test.

As the discussion about Britishness and immigration went on, it became clear that the government believed, as the Green Paper of July 2008 said, that:

> *A clearer understanding of the rights and responsibilities that go with British citizenship will help build our sense of shared identity and social cohesion.*

This definition of 'Britishness' came down, in the end, simply to obeying the law.

Images of Britishness

Last Night of the Proms: waving the Union Jack; singing 'Rule Britannia' and 'Jerusalem'.

A businessman: correct; smart; stiff upper-lip; reserved.

Love of the monarchy and of British history and traditions.

The Houses of Parliament: democracy and freedom.

The English landscape: the Lake District; quiet country villages; Miss Marple; cricket; afternoon tea.

Fish and chips; Blackpool; kiss-me-quick hats; sandcastles; ice creams.

Multi-racial; multi-faith; multi-cultural; multi-agency; multi-media.

Activities

1. Looking at the images of Britishness on this page, discuss:
   a) Images 1–6 give very traditional views of Britishness. How relevant are they to your experience of what it is to be 'British'?
   b) Do any of the images 1–6 exclude parts of the population?
   c) Is image 7 a more relevant image of Britishness? Why?
2. Working as a group, discuss what the word 'Britishness' means to you. Design a poster or an image to show your idea.
3. If you had to devise a 'British citizenship' test, what questions would you ask?

Plenary: Taking sides

Debate: Should immigration be stopped?

Arguments that 'IMMIGRATION SHOULD BE STOPPED'

1. Contrary to the common belief, there have always in the past been only very small numbers of immigrants – we are *not* a 'mongrel nation' and, genetically, most British people are similar.

2. The massive inflow of immigrants in the last three decades has significantly damaged traditional 'British' culture.

3. We cannot afford millions more immigrants; it is a crazy notion that a nation of 50 million people can open its border to 500 million Europeans and billions from elsewhere on earth. We are already one of the most crowded countries in the world.

4. Most British people think that there are too many immigrants.

5. Historically, immigrants have always been treated badly and subjected to racism; it is difficult to see why anybody would *want* to come and live here.

6. By allowing immigrants to work here as cheap labour, Britain is taking advantage of them.

7. Britain is stealing the poorest nations' most skilled labourers – this is morally wrong.

8. Allowing mass immigration helps the growth of right-wing, racist and neo-Nazi groups; it puts strains on community cohesion, and sometimes leads to violence.

9. Trying to assimilate to the British way of life also puts intolerable strain on immigrant families – some individuals become so alienated that they plant bombs.

10. Anyone who thinks 'Inglan is a bitch' ought simply to go back to their country of origin.

Activities – Debate

1. Divide the class into two groups: 'for' and 'against' stopping immigration. Working with a friend from the same group, discuss the ideas on pages 46–47 which support 'your' case. Try to find, in this book, facts which prove the points.

2. Looking back through this book, think of some other points to make about whether immigration should be stopped or not.

3. Coming together as a whole class, debate the following: Should immigration be stopped?

Arguments that 'IMMIGRATION SHOULD NOT BE STOPPED'

1. All Britons are immigrants – if you go back far enough.

2. Whether we like it or not, Britain has been a mongrel, magpie nation since time began, always adopting immigrants, their skills and their ideas.

3. Immigrants have contributed an incalculable amount of culture, ideas, wealth and vitality to this nation, without which it would not be what it has been and is today.

4. The inclusion of ethnic communities and cultures has widened, improved and benefited our lifestyle beyond measure. It is hypocrisy to enjoy a curry and then say Britain ought to stop immigration.

5. 'Britain is by far – and I mean *by far* – the best place in Europe to live if you are not white.' (Trevor Phillips, Chairman of the Commission for Racial Equality.)

6. Immigrant workers are essential, and will become more so as the population grows older.

7. It is Britain's humanitarian and moral duty, as a rich, free country, to open its borders to those who are starving and oppressed.

8. Anti-immigrant racism is degrading and intolerable; Britain has a moral duty to be more tolerant and accepting.

9. Britishness is a joke – there is no such thing; Britain is merely the collection through history of all its different immigrant cultures, and Britishness will continue to change as new people arrive.

10. Many immigrants love Britain, and are grateful for the opportunity Britain has given them; that does not mean they have to put up with discrimination, racism or injustice.

Activities – Summing it all up

1. On pages 4–5, at the beginning of this course, you were asked to suggest a caption for this photograph. Look back at what you wrote. At the end of the course, do you still feel that your caption is appropriate? If not, think of a new, better-informed caption.
2. On page 5 you were also asked to write down your 'First thoughts on immigration'. Look back at what you wrote. At the end of the course, do you still agree with what you wrote?
3. If you had to sum up your thoughts about immigration now, what would you say? Write down your new, better-informed ideas in less than 50 words.

Understanding: How significant has immigration been?

◄ Illegal immigration: This CCTV picture shows the lorry of Dutch driver Perry Wacker going through Dover customs in June 2000. Hidden in the lorry were 58 Chinese illegal immigrants.

To try to avoid detection, Wacker had closed the air vents. When the doors were opened all 58 people were found suffocated. Wacker was jailed for 14 years on 58 counts of manslaughter and conspiracy to smuggle illegal immigrants into Britain.

Significance involves five ideas. An issue is historically significant if:

1 Studying it tells you a lot about history.
How much have you learned about Britain's past by studying immigration? Scan back through the book and select TWO important facts you have learned.

2 It had a big effect.
Search back through the book (especially pages 7–8, 12–21, 24, 32–34 and 42–43) looking for the effects of immigration. Choose TWO consequences you feel have been especially important.

3 It was important at the time.
Scan back through the book (for example pages 10, 23, 25, 27, 31, 33, 36–37 and 38). Find TWO good examples of facts or sources which give the impression that people *in the past* thought that immigration was important.

4 People still regard it as important.
I suppose the fact that you are studying it now proves they do! But *how* important is the history of immigration now? Find TWO clues from pages 5, 9, 40–41 and 44–45.

5 It raises issues which still mean something today.
Scan back through the book and find TWO issues which this study of immigration raised in your mind. Discuss with the class or a friend how relevant these issues are to us, in our world, today.

Activities – How significant was immigration?

1. How does the picture above confirm that immigration was still an important issue at the start of the twenty-first century?
2. Using the ideas and information from this page, have a class discussion about how significant a historical topic immigration is.
3. Have you ENJOYED studying the history of immigration?